Bilingual Edition
READING POWER
Edición Bilingüe

Extreme Machines

Powerboats

Lanchas motorizadas

Scott P. Werther

The Rosen Publishing Group's
PowerKids Press™ & Buenas Letras™
New York

1

Published in 2003 by The Rosen Publishing Group, Inc.
29 East 21st Street, New York, NY 10010
Copyright © 2003 by The Rosen Publishing Group, Inc.

First Bilingual Edition 2003
First Edition in English 2002

Book Design: Michelle Innes
Photo Credits: Cover © Forest Johnson/Corbis; pp. 4–5 © Index Stock;
p. 7 © Tim Bieber/Image Bank; p. 9 © Bill Schild/Corbis;
p. 11 © Mike Powell/Allsport; pp. 12–13 © Yann Guichaoua/Allsport; pp.
14–15 © Robert Holland/Image Bank; pp. 16–17 © The Purcell
Team/Corbis; p. 19 © Forest Johnson/Corbis; pp. 20–21 © Phil
Schermeister/Corbis

Werther , Scott P
Powerboats/Lanchas motorizadas/Scott P. Werther ; traducción al español:
Spanish Educational Publishing
p. cm. — (Extreme Machines)
Includes bibliographical references and index.
ISBN 0-8239-6890-1 (lib. bdg.)
1. Motorboats—Juvenile literature. [1. Motorboats 2. Spanish Language
Materials—Bilingual.] I. Title.
TG106.K63 T48 2001
624'.5—dc21

2001000599

Manufactured in the United States of America

Contents

Contenido

3

This is a powerboat. It is one of the fastest boats on the water.

Ésta es una lancha motorizada.
Es uno de los barcos más veloces.

Powerboats can travel as fast as a car. They can go 60 miles (96.5km) an hour.

Las lanchas motorizadas avanzan tan rápido como un auto. Pueden navegar a 60 millas (96.5km) por hora. .

Powerboats are steered the
same way as a car.

———————————

Las lanchas motorizadas
se manejan igual que un auto.

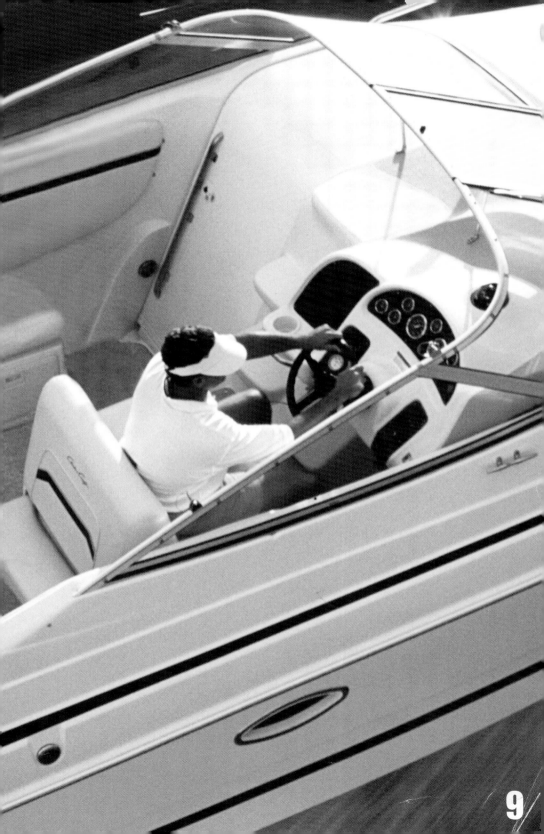

Powerboats have big engines
to go fast.

Para avanzar rápido,
las lanchas motorizadas
tienen un motor grande.

The engine of a powerboat
has a propeller.

El motor de las lanchas
motorizadas tiene una hélice.

Propeller

Hélice

13

The engine turns the propeller.
The propeller spins in the water
and moves the powerboat
very fast.

El motor hace girar la hélice.
La hélice gira en el agua
y hace que la lancha avance
muy rápido.

Many people use powerboats. The United States Coast Guard uses powerboats to help save people in danger on the sea.

Muchas personas usan lanchas
motorizadas.
El Servicio de Guardacostas
usa lanchas motorizadas
para ayudar a las personas
que corren peligro en el mar.

People also use powerboats for fun. Water-skiers are pulled by powerboats.

También usamos las lanchas motorizadas para divertirnos. Las usamos para esquiar sobre el agua.

Powerboats can be enjoyed by people of all ages.

Grandes y chicos disfrutan
de las lanchas motorizadas.

Glossary

Coast Guard (kohst gard) the branch of the armed forces that protects people and property along U.S. coasts

engine (ehn-juhn) a machine that changes fuel into motion and power

propeller (pruh-**pehl**-uhr) metal blades that spin in the water and move a boat forward

steer (stihr) to make something go in a particular direction

water-skier (waw-tuhr **skee**-uhr) someone who glides over the water on water skis while being pulled by a powerboat

Glosario

esquiar sobre el agua deporte en que la persona se desliza con esquís sobre el agua, agarrándose de una cuerda que está atada a una lancha motorizada

hélice (la) cuchillas de metal que giran en el agua y hacen que el barco se mueva hacia adelante

manejar hacer que algo vaya en una dirección

motor (el) máquina que transforma el combustible en movimiento y potencia

Servicio de Guardacostas (el) rama de las fuerzas armadas que protege a las personas y la propiedad en las costas de los Estados Unidos

Resources / Recursos

Here are more books to read about powerboats:
Otros libros que puedes leer sobre lanchas motorizadas:

Boats
by Ian S. Graham
Raintree/Steck Vaughn (1999)

Eyewitness: Boat
by Eric Kentley
Dorling Kindersley, New York (2000)

Web sites
Due to the changing nature of Internet links, PowerKids Press has developed an online list of Web sites related to the subject of this book. This site is updated regularly. Please use this link to access the list:

Sitios web
Debido a las constantes modificaciones en los sitios de Internet, PowerKids Press ha desarrollado una guía on-line de sitios relacionados al tema de este libro. Nuestro sitio web se actualiza constantemente. Por favor utiliza la siguiente dirección para consultar la lista:

http://www.buenasletraslinks.com/chl/tmb

Word count in English: 111
Número de palabras en español: 124

Index

Índice